Rex Rat is having a birthday party.

Today he is six.

He wants to have cake and lemonade.

He will play tag.

This is the game he likes best.

His friends Fred Frog and Pat Pig will

come. But he is not sure his best friend,

Sal Snake, will come.

4

Rex and Sal were in the mud this morning.

Rex had the rake.

Sal had the spade so she

could plant  .

Rex said, "Let's trade so I can

plant ."

Sal said, "No, I want the spade!"

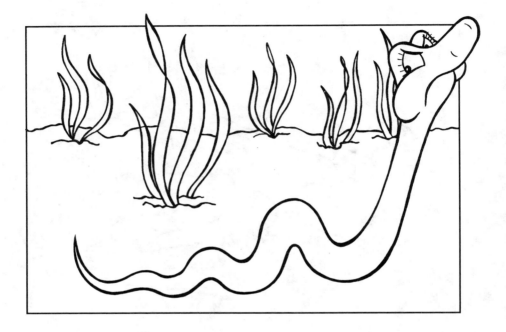

Sal went to her house mad.

Rex went to his house mad.

Tap, tap, tap.

"Who is it?" said Rex.

"Let's be friends," said Sal.

"Happy, happy birthday, Rex Rat!"

Write or Draw

Who is your best friend?